The Cigar Log Book

by

Nathan Scott Lester

Printed and made in the U.S.A. on acid-free paper stock supplied by a Forest Stewardship Council-certified provider. Interior paper is made from 30% post-consumer waste recycled material.

Illustrations and design by Nathan Scott Lester

Edited by Tracy Lester

Photographs by Holly Baumann Photography
http://www.hollybaumannphotography.com

ISBN-13:   978-0-9845825-0-1

First Edition

10 9 8 7 6 5 4 3 2 1

to you and your cigars

Preferred Tobacconist Information

Name _____

Phone _____

Address _____

Email _____

Hours _____

Web _____

Name _____

Phone _____

Address _____

Email _____

Hours _____

Web _____

Name _____

Phone _____

Address _____

Email _____

Hours _____

Web _____

TABLE OF CONTENTS

Respite

A cigar offers me a respite from today's everyday hustle. Taking time to enjoy a fine handmade cigar is my reprieve from a hectic week.

I examine the cigar's structure and admire the silky, flawless wrapping. I perform the ritual of puncturing the cap and lighting the foot similar to a sommelier opening a bottle of fine wine. As the initial embers grow around the cigar, I inhale the tobacco's wafting aroma.

With my first draw, my stresses begin to fade as I dream about the tobacco's journey from seed to cigar. I imagine the bright sun and warm dry air rustling the leaves prior to harvest, the cedar lined rooms full with bales of aging and fermenting tobaccos, and the master blender's secret recipe being sorted, bunched and rolled with skilled precision by the roller's hands.

I sit and enjoy the effort and artistry that offers me the opportunity for reflection, relaxation and rejuvenation.

INTRODUCTION

Better to have a dull pencil than a sharp mind.
- English Proverb -

The Cigar Log Book provides cigar enthusiasts a place to record tasting experiences as well as a place to collect cigar bands (I call them, *cigart*). The beginning pages include a brief description of anatomy, production, structure, shape, taste, and choice. The majority of the pages contain cigar entry logs allowing you to evaluate cigars and document your experiences. *The Cigar Log Book* helps you to identify your cigar palate in order to make the right choice when visiting your local tobacconist.

CIGAR ANATOMY

The anatomy, or structure, of a cigar includes the foot (end you light), body, head (end you puff) and cap (the cover you cut or punch). The makeup of a cigar's structure comes from three main components: filler, binder and wrapper.

FILLER

Filler is the bulk of a cigar and is made by compacting a number of tobacco leaves together. A master cigar roller knows the proper filler density needed for a premium cigar's easy and consistent draw through the entire cigar length. If a cigar's

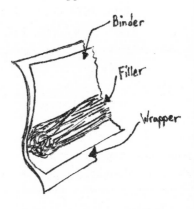

filler is too dense, smoking the cigar is like pulling a thick milkshake through a straw. If the filler is too loose or spongy, the cigar becomes hot and harsh as you draw and could burn out. Both too tight and too loose renders an otherwise good cigar futile. Like Goldilocks, you want your cigar filler just right.

BINDER

Binder holds the filler together in the cigar's final shape. The binder leaves are often wrapper leaves that didn't make the final cut because of blemishes and discolorations. Some cigar makers use bold, spicy, or sweet binders as a way to impart additional flavors and taste complexity without overpowering the filler. The binder makes up a minimal volume of the entire cigar when compared to the filler.

WRAPPER

Wrapper leaves are the pinnacle of the tobacco plant. Because the wrapper leaves make up such a small portion of the cigar, little flavor is imparted to the tasting experience. Wrapper leaves provide visual beauty and go through a rigorous inspection process. From the creamy, smooth Connecticut to the textured and dark African Camaroon, nothing is more prized than a cigar's wrapper.

FROM SEED TO CIGAR

Analogous to grapes for a fine wine, tobacco for a premium cigar requires stellar growing conditions, proper soil, fine tobacco seed and experienced growers. Tobacco seeds for premium cigars are grown mostly in sunny, tropical climates. Seeds are planted on farms or vegas and tended to by vegueros or tobacco farmers.

Most of the cigar bulk comes from tobacco plants grown outdoors in full sunlight. A plant may take two or three months to mature and typically contains fewer than 20 leaves. Tobacco leaf flavor increases from the base (volado) to top (ligero) of the plant, and harvesting involves picking a few leaves at a time from the volado up.

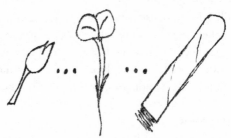

The wrapper leaves typically come from tobacco plants grown in muslin tents. These tents help protect the leaves from the scorching sun and other harsh conditions. This produces a leaf devoid of blemishes, discolorations and other cosmetic defects. Due to the strict inspection process, very few leaves become wrapper leaves.

DRYING AND PRIMARY FERMENTATION
Once tobacco leaves have been plucked from the plant, they are bunched and hung to dry for approximately 1 ½ months.

These bunches are then placed into stacks to ferment between 1 – 1 ½ months. Fermentation helps stabilize color elements in the leaves and helps extract oils, tar, nicotine and other impurities.

AGING AND SORTING

After the leaves have been initially fermented they are collected into bales and wrapped in burlap for storage. Much like the fermentation process, aging helps mellow some of the tobacco's harsh components and reduce nicotine and tar to levels enjoyable without ill feeling . This step can take as long as 2 years. After aging the leaves, the stems are removed and sorted according to color, size and texture.

SECONDARY FERMENTATION AND AGING

Depending on the cigar's tobacco classification, the tobacco is fermented a second time between 1 ½ – 2 months. Just as in primary fermentation, this secondary fermentation helps to eliminate impurities in the tobacco and to homogenize flavors among all the tobacco leaves.

After secondary fermentation is complete, tobacco is packaged in bundles and covered to be aged. This aging can take as long as 3 years before the tobacco is delivered to the cigar factory. Some cigar filler tobacco may be aged and fermented for additional years after delivery to the cigar rolling factory.

BLENDING, ROLLING AND WRAPPING

Each cigar has its own particular blend of tobacco or recipe. Once the tobacco filler has been blended to the proper recipe, the cigar is formed in the desired shape, wrapped with a binder leaf and placed in a mold awaiting its final wrapper. After receiving a dress of wrapper leaves, the cigar is closed and cut to length.

WHERE'S YOUR CIGAR FROM?

Some people say that cigars from Cuba are superior. Whether true or not, there is a definite aura around the famed Cuban cigar for many Americans. Due to the U.S. Trade Embargo established in 1962, it is illegal for any American to purchase or have a Cuban cigar on American soil. Luckily for Americans, there are many countries besides Cuba considered by aficionados as major producers of top rated tobacco and cigars. These other countries have ideal terroir, or soil and climates for producing premium tobacco. Some of these countries have been producing premium and super-premium cigars for decades. These countries, in no particular order, include but are not limited to, Mexico, Honduras, Nicaragua and the Dominican Republic.

Where a cigar is made does not necessarily mean a cigar's tobacco is exclusively from that country. It is common to purchase a cigar made of several tobaccos from various countries. These "blends" of tobacco impart their own taste influences and are key to a master blender's recipe providing enjoyers of cigars a mélange of top notch choices.

KNOW YOUR VITOLA (SIZE AND SHAPE)

The cigar makers have blessed this great world with a variety of sizes and shapes giving cigar enjoyers a veritable cornucopia of options for any situation. Cigar makers in their infinite wisdom have created smaller cigars for those on the go to larger versions for enjoying during all day activities like barbeques. Whatever your discretion there are two major categories of cigars in regards to shape, Parejo or Corona and Figurado.

PAREJO
Parejo or Corona – This shape is the most common form. The Parejo is cylindrical in shape with a rounded capped end that is

to be pierced, notched or cut off prior to smoking. Parejos have many lengths and girths as shown in Table 1 below.

Table 1: Common vitola for Parejo cigars.

Common Name	Length (inches)	Ring Gauge (64th an inch)
Panatela	5 ½ - 6 ½	34 - 38
Robusto	4 ½ - 5	48 - 50
Corona	5 ½ - 6	42 - 45
Lonsdale	6 - 6 ½	42 - 44
Churchill	6 ½ - 7	46 - 48
Double Corona	7 ½ - 8	48 - 52
Presidente	7 - 8 ½	52 - 60

FIGURADO

Figurado – These cigars are considered more difficult to make, which causes some to feel they are a more prestigious cigar. Figurados, as shown in Table 2 below, include various forms and one of the more popular vitola is the Torpedo.

Table 2: Common vitola for Figurado cigars.

Common Name	Length (inches)	Ring Gauge (64th an inch)
Torpedo*	5 ½ - 6 ½	46 - 52
Perfecto	5 - 6	50 - 52
Belicoso†	5 ½ - 6 ½	48 - 52
Pyramid*	6 - 6 ½	46 - 52

Many use the terms Torpedo and Pyramid interchangeably however some differentiate the two. Torpedos are very similar to the Parejo style cigar except their head comes to a point while the Pyramid has a similar pointed cap and continues to grow in girth from the pointed cap to the open end.

†The Belicoso is shaped like a Pyramid but has a rounded head rather than a pointed one.

TASTE IS EVERYTHING

When not flavored, a cigar's taste comes from the blend of tobaccos and the storage. The tobacco's flavor comes from the soil and climate where the tobacco was grown and the aging and fermentation process of the leaves after harvest. A master blender's cigar tobacco blend is a trade secret and gives each cigar line its unique taste. Cigars from the same line contain the same blend giving the enjoyer of any vitola in that line generally the same taste. For instance, smoking a *La Perla Habana's Morado* Robusto will likely taste the same as a *La Perla Habana's Morado* Torpedo as long as they have been properly stored.

A cigar's taste can vary from light, mild, heavy, to full-bodied, which can be attributed to an increasing amount of tar and nicotine in the tobacco leaves. Pay attention to the cigar's taste for the duration of your cigar respite. A cigar can take on different taste characteristics throughout the experience. Some cigars are made so the beginning has a mild taste and becomes more full-bodied the further you go. Unfortunately, though rare with premium cigars, some cigars start out with a smooth complex taste only to become bitter and acrid halfway through. A great cigar is held to a higher standard and can be enjoyed all the way to the nub.

When tasting a cigar, much like a fine wine, it is important to note the complexities. Some words used to describe cigar taste are smooth, vegetative, musty, bitter, creamy, acrid, light, powerful, spicy and peppery.

CHOOSING A CIGAR

Choosing a cigar is personal and subjective. Foremost, you must ensure your cigar is handmade or "Hecho a Mano" using long-filler tobacco. You can find these from a trustworthy tobacconist. Machine made cigars are typically made from short-filler scrap tobacco that did not make the cut for a premium handmade cigar.

Choosing a cigar can depend on mood, company and a variety of other things. In today's hectic environment, many times your choice will be based on schedule and mood. It is important to know the various sizes and shapes of cigars to match the time you have. It is equally important to know the body of various cigars to match your mood or company. A mild, smooth Presidente cigar may be more appropriate for relaxing in the backyard with a light beer while a full-bodied, Robusto cigar may be good as you walk your dog after a heavy dinner.

When choosing a cigar, one should note a cigar's country of origin does not indicate a premium or lesser quality. It would also be a mistake to assume a cigar's origination determines the cigar's body. Many countries that have been known to make milder cigars have been producing serious full-bodied cigars for years. It is best to do a bit of research on the web or at your local tobacconist's shop when choosing a cigar for the first time.

CIGAR LOG ENTRIES

The following pages allow you to record important data regarding your cigar and experience. The list below gives direction for each component of *The Cigar Log Book* entries.

Minutiae: Minor cigar details.

Vitola: The shape name, gauge and length of your cigar. In the back of this book there is a page with various ring gauges and a ruler to measure your cigars.

Anatomy: Here you can record the country(ies) of origin and the various tobaccos that comprise your cigar.

Appearance: Is your cigar dry or oily, light or dark, thick veins or smooth complexion? Record the visual appearance.

Construction: Is your cigar firm with a slight give throughout the length or is it spongy in places? Is the cap constructed seamlessly or is it misshapen? Record how you think the roller did when making your cigar.

Draw: How is the draw on the cigar when you take a puff? Is it difficult, too easy or just right? Record at the start, halfway and three-quarters of the way through.

Burn: Is your cigar burning evenly at the foot or unevenly creating a "canoe"? Record this at the start, halfway and three-quarters of the way through.

Tasting Notes: Make note of any flavors or tastes you get from the draw and the wrapper (spicy, musty, smooth, leathery, toasty, etc.).

Other Notes: Here you can log any other notes or things you notice about the cigar such as "Pairs well with cognac" or "The aroma was killing flies." You can also choose to comment on the ash structure and tobacco's aroma.

Evaluation: Is the cigar poor and needs to be thrown away never to be enjoyed again? If so, fill **1** "cigar ring" on the poor end of the 1 to 10 rating section of the cigar log entry. Is the cigar a knock your socks off pleasurable experience? Fill all **10** "cigar rings" for a "Classic" rating. Okay but nothing great? Fill **5** "cigar rings." You get the idea.

Recommend and enjoy again: Just in case you were unaware, **Y** is yes and **N** is no.

Cigar Log Entry

MINUTIAE	DATE		OCCASION	
BRAND				PRICE
VITOLA	GAUGE		LENGTH	
SHAPE NAME				
ANATOMY	FILLER			
BINDER			WRAPPER	
APPEARANCE				

CONSTRUCTION

DRAW	START	1/2	3/4
BURN	START	1/2	3/4

TASTING NOTES

OTHER NOTES

EVALUATION

O O O O O O O O O O

POOR   CLASSIC

RECOMMEND AND ENJOY AGAIN?   Y   N

Cigar Log Entry

MINUTIAE	DATE	OCCASION	
BRAND			PRICE
VITOLA	GAUGE	LENGTH	
SHAPE NAME			
ANATOMY	FILLER		
BINDER		WRAPPER	
APPEARANCE			

CONSTRUCTION

DRAW	START	1/2	3/4
BURN	START	1/2	3/4

TASTING NOTES

OTHER NOTES

EVALUATION

◯ ◯ ◯ ◯ ◯ ◯ ◯ ◯ ◯ ◯

POOR   CLASSIC

RECOMMEND AND ENJOY AGAIN?   Y   N

ATTACH BAND HERE

Cigar Log Entry

```
ATTACH BAND HERE
```

MINUTIAE	DATE		OCCASION		
BRAND					PRICE
VITOLA	GAUGE		LENGTH		
SHAPE NAME					
ANATOMY	FILLER				
BINDER			WRAPPER		

APPEARANCE

CONSTRUCTION

DRAW	START	1/2	3/4
BURN	START	1/2	3/4

TASTING NOTES

OTHER NOTES

EVALUATION

O O O O O O O O O O

POOR   CLASSIC

RECOMMEND AND ENJOY AGAIN?   Y   N

Cigar Log Entry

MINUTIAE	DATE		OCCASION		
BRAND					PRICE
VITOLA	GAUGE		LENGTH		
SHAPE NAME					
ANATOMY	FILLER				
BINDER			WRAPPER		
APPEARANCE					
CONSTRUCTION					

DRAW	START	1/2	3/4
BURN	START	1/2	3/4

TASTING NOTES

OTHER NOTES

EVALUATION

O O O O O O O O O O

POOR   CLASSIC

RECOMMEND AND ENJOY AGAIN?   Y   N

ATTACH BAND HERE

Cigar Log Entry

ATTACH BAND HERE

MINUTIAE	DATE		OCCASION		
BRAND				PRICE	
VITOLA	GAUGE		LENGTH		
SHAPE NAME					
ANATOMY	FILLER				
BINDER			WRAPPER		
APPEARANCE					
CONSTRUCTION					
DRAW	START	1/2		3/4	
BURN	START	1/2		3/4	

TASTING NOTES

OTHER NOTES

EVALUATION

O O O O O O O O O O

POOR   CLASSIC

RECOMMEND AND ENJOY AGAIN?   Y   N

Cigar Log Entry

MINUTIAE	DATE		OCCASION		
BRAND					PRICE
VITOLA	GAUGE		LENGTH		
SHAPE NAME					
ANATOMY	FILLER				
BINDER			WRAPPER		
APPEARANCE					
CONSTRUCTION					

DRAW	START	1/2	3/4
BURN	START	1/2	3/4

TASTING NOTES

OTHER NOTES

EVALUATION

O O O O O O O O O O

POOR   CLASSIC

RECOMMEND AND ENJOY AGAIN?   Y   N

ATTACH BAND HERE

Cigar Log Entry

ATTACH BAND HERE

MINUTIAE	DATE		OCCASION		
BRAND				PRICE	
VITOLA	GAUGE		LENGTH		
SHAPE NAME					
ANATOMY	FILLER				
BINDER			WRAPPER		
APPEARANCE					
CONSTRUCTION					
DRAW	START		1/2		3/4
BURN	START		1/2		3/4

TASTING NOTES

OTHER NOTES

EVALUATION

O O O O O O O O O O

POOR   CLASSIC

RECOMMEND AND ENJOY AGAIN?   Y   N

Cigar Log Entry

MINUTIAE	DATE		OCCASION		
BRAND					PRICE
VITOLA	GAUGE			LENGTH	
SHAPE NAME					
ANATOMY	FILLER				
BINDER			WRAPPER		

APPEARANCE

CONSTRUCTION

DRAW	START		1/2		3/4
BURN	START		1/2		3/4

TASTING NOTES

OTHER NOTES

EVALUATION

○ ○ ○ ○ ○ ○ ○ ○ ○ ○

POOR   CLASSIC

RECOMMEND AND ENJOY AGAIN?   Y   N

ATTACH BAND HERE

Cigar Log Entry

ATTACH BAND HERE

MINUTIAE	DATE		OCCASION		
BRAND					PRICE
VITOLA	GAUGE		LENGTH		
SHAPE NAME					
ANATOMY	FILLER				
BINDER			WRAPPER		
APPEARANCE					
CONSTRUCTION					
DRAW	START	1/2		3/4	
BURN	START	1/2		3/4	

TASTING NOTES

OTHER NOTES

EVALUATION

O O O O O O O O O O

POOR   CLASSIC

RECOMMEND AND ENJOY AGAIN?   Y   N

Cigar Log Entry

MINUTIAE	DATE		OCCASION		
BRAND					PRICE
VITOLA	GAUGE		LENGTH		
SHAPE NAME					
ANATOMY	FILLER				
BINDER			WRAPPER		

APPEARANCE

CONSTRUCTION

DRAW	START	1/2	3/4
BURN	START	1/2	3/4

TASTING NOTES

OTHER NOTES

EVALUATION

O O O O O O O O O O

POOR   CLASSIC

RECOMMEND AND ENJOY AGAIN?   Y   N

ATTACH BAND HERE

Cigar Log Entry

ATTACH BAND HERE

MINUTIAE	DATE	OCCASION	

BRAND			PRICE

VITOLA	GAUGE		LENGTH

SHAPE NAME

ANATOMY	FILLER

BINDER		WRAPPER

APPEARANCE

CONSTRUCTION

DRAW	START	1/2	3/4
BURN	START	1/2	3/4

TASTING NOTES

OTHER NOTES

EVALUATION

O O O O O O O O O O

POOR   CLASSIC

RECOMMEND AND ENJOY AGAIN?   Y   N

Cigar Log Entry

MINUTIAE	DATE	OCCASION	
BRAND			PRICE
VITOLA	GAUGE		LENGTH
SHAPE NAME			
ANATOMY	FILLER		
BINDER		WRAPPER	
APPEARANCE			
CONSTRUCTION			

DRAW	START	1/2	3/4
BURN	START	1/2	3/4

TASTING NOTES

OTHER NOTES

EVALUATION

O O O O O O O O O O

POOR   CLASSIC

RECOMMEND AND ENJOY AGAIN?   Y   N

ATTACH BAND HERE

Cigar Log Entry

ATTACH BAND HERE

MINUTIAE	DATE		OCCASION		
BRAND				PRICE	
VITOLA	GAUGE		LENGTH		
SHAPE NAME					
ANATOMY	FILLER				
BINDER			WRAPPER		
APPEARANCE					
CONSTRUCTION					
DRAW	START	1/2		3/4	
BURN	START	1/2		3/4	

TASTING NOTES

OTHER NOTES

EVALUATION

O O O O O O O O O O

POOR   CLASSIC

RECOMMEND AND ENJOY AGAIN?   Y   N

Cigar Log Entry

MINUTIAE	DATE		OCCASION		
BRAND					PRICE
VITOLA	GAUGE		LENGTH		
SHAPE NAME					
ANATOMY	FILLER				
BINDER			WRAPPER		
APPEARANCE					
CONSTRUCTION					
DRAW	START	1/2		3/4	
BURN	START	1/2		3/4	

TASTING NOTES

OTHER NOTES

EVALUATION

O O O O O O O O O O

POOR   CLASSIC

RECOMMEND AND ENJOY AGAIN?   Y   N

ATTACH BAND HERE

Cigar Log Entry

ATTACH BAND HERE

MINUTIAE	DATE		OCCASION	
BRAND				PRICE
VITOLA	GAUGE		LENGTH	
SHAPE NAME				
ANATOMY	FILLER			
BINDER			WRAPPER	

APPEARANCE

CONSTRUCTION

DRAW	START	1/2	3/4
BURN	START	1/2	3/4

TASTING NOTES

OTHER NOTES

EVALUATION

○ ○ ○ ○ ○ ○ ○ ○ ○ ○

POOR   CLASSIC

RECOMMEND AND ENJOY AGAIN?   Y   N

Cigar Log Entry

MINUTIAE	DATE	OCCASION	

BRAND			PRICE

VITOLA	GAUGE		LENGTH	

SHAPE NAME				

ANATOMY	FILLER			

BINDER		WRAPPER	

APPEARANCE

CONSTRUCTION

DRAW	START		1/2		3/4
BURN	START		1/2		3/4

TASTING NOTES

OTHER NOTES

EVALUATION

O O O O O O O O O O

POOR   CLASSIC

RECOMMEND AND ENJOY AGAIN?   Y   N

ATTACH BAND HERE

Cigar Log Entry

ATTACH BAND HERE

MINUTIAE	DATE	OCCASION	

BRAND			PRICE

VITOLA	GAUGE		LENGTH

SHAPE NAME

ANATOMY	FILLER	

BINDER		WRAPPER

APPEARANCE

CONSTRUCTION

DRAW	START	1/2	3/4
BURN	START	1/2	3/4

TASTING NOTES

OTHER NOTES

EVALUATION

O O O O O O O O O O

POOR   CLASSIC

RECOMMEND AND ENJOY AGAIN?   Y   N

Cigar Log Entry

MINUTIAE	DATE		OCCASION		
BRAND					PRICE
VITOLA	GAUGE			LENGTH	
SHAPE NAME					
ANATOMY	FILLER				
BINDER			WRAPPER		
APPEARANCE					
CONSTRUCTION					

DRAW	START		1/2		3/4
BURN	START		1/2		3/4

TASTING NOTES

OTHER NOTES

EVALUATION

⭕ ⭕ ⭕ ⭕ ⭕ ⭕ ⭕ ⭕ ⭕ ⭕

POOR   CLASSIC

RECOMMEND AND ENJOY AGAIN?   Y   N

ATTACH BAND HERE

Cigar Log Entry

ATTACH BAND HERE

MINUTIAE	DATE	OCCASION	

BRAND			PRICE

VITOLA	GAUGE	LENGTH	

SHAPE NAME

ANATOMY	FILLER		

BINDER		WRAPPER	

APPEARANCE

CONSTRUCTION

DRAW	START	1/2	3/4
BURN	START	1/2	3/4

TASTING NOTES

OTHER NOTES

EVALUATION

○ ○ ○ ○ ○ ○ ○ ○ ○ ○

POOR CLASSIC

RECOMMEND AND ENJOY AGAIN? Y N

Cigar Log Entry

MINUTIAE	DATE		OCCASION		
BRAND					PRICE
VITOLA	GAUGE		LENGTH		
SHAPE NAME					
ANATOMY	FILLER				
BINDER			WRAPPER		
APPEARANCE					
CONSTRUCTION					

DRAW	START	1/2	3/4
BURN	START	1/2	3/4

TASTING NOTES

OTHER NOTES

EVALUATION

O O O O O O O O O O

POOR   CLASSIC

RECOMMEND AND ENJOY AGAIN?   Y   N

ATTACH BAND HERE

Cigar Log Entry

ATTACH BAND HERE

MINUTIAE	DATE		OCCASION		
BRAND					PRICE
VITOLA	GAUGE		LENGTH		
SHAPE NAME					
ANATOMY	FILLER				
BINDER			WRAPPER		
APPEARANCE					
CONSTRUCTION					
DRAW	START	1/2		3/4	
BURN	START	1/2		3/4	

TASTING NOTES

OTHER NOTES

EVALUATION

O O O O O O O O O O

POOR   CLASSIC

RECOMMEND AND ENJOY AGAIN?   Y   N

Cigar Log Entry

MINUTIAE	DATE		OCCASION		
BRAND					PRICE
VITOLA	GAUGE		LENGTH		
SHAPE NAME					
ANATOMY	FILLER				
BINDER			WRAPPER		
APPEARANCE					
CONSTRUCTION					

DRAW	START	1/2	3/4
BURN	START	1/2	3/4

TASTING NOTES

OTHER NOTES

EVALUATION

O O O O O O O O O O

POOR CLASSIC

RECOMMEND AND ENJOY AGAIN? Y N

ATTACH BAND HERE

Cigar Log Entry

ATTACH BAND HERE

MINUTIAE	DATE		OCCASION		
BRAND					PRICE
VITOLA	GAUGE		LENGTH		
SHAPE NAME					
ANATOMY	FILLER				
BINDER			WRAPPER		
APPEARANCE					
CONSTRUCTION					

DRAW	START	1/2	3/4
BURN	START	1/2	3/4

TASTING NOTES

OTHER NOTES

EVALUATION

○ ○ ○ ○ ○ ○ ○ ○ ○ ○

POOR   CLASSIC

RECOMMEND AND ENJOY AGAIN?   Y   N

Cigar Log Entry

MINUTIAE	DATE		OCCASION		
BRAND					PRICE
VITOLA	GAUGE		LENGTH		
SHAPE NAME					
ANATOMY	FILLER				
BINDER			WRAPPER		
APPEARANCE					
CONSTRUCTION					

DRAW	START	1/2	3/4
BURN	START	1/2	3/4

TASTING NOTES

OTHER NOTES

EVALUATION

○ ○ ○ ○ ○ ○ ○ ○ ○ ○

POOR   CLASSIC

RECOMMEND AND ENJOY AGAIN?   Y   N

ATTACH BAND HERE

Cigar Log Entry

```
ATTACH BAND HERE
```

MINUTIAE	DATE		OCCASION		
BRAND				PRICE	
VITOLA	GAUGE		LENGTH		
SHAPE NAME					
ANATOMY	FILLER				
BINDER			WRAPPER		
APPEARANCE					
CONSTRUCTION					
DRAW	START	1/2		3/4	
BURN	START	1/2		3/4	

TASTING NOTES

OTHER NOTES

EVALUATION

○ ○ ○ ○ ○ ○ ○ ○ ○ ○

POOR   CLASSIC

RECOMMEND AND ENJOY AGAIN?   Y   N

Cigar Log Entry

MINUTIAE	DATE		OCCASION		
BRAND					PRICE
VITOLA	GAUGE		LENGTH		
SHAPE NAME					
ANATOMY	FILLER				
BINDER			WRAPPER		

APPEARANCE

CONSTRUCTION

DRAW	START	1/2	3/4
BURN	START	1/2	3/4

TASTING NOTES

OTHER NOTES

EVALUATION

O O O O O O O O O O

POOR   CLASSIC

RECOMMEND AND ENJOY AGAIN?   Y   N

ATTACH BAND HERE

Cigar Log Entry

ATTACH BAND HERE

MINUTIAE	DATE	OCCASION	

BRAND			PRICE

VITOLA	GAUGE	LENGTH	

SHAPE NAME

ANATOMY	FILLER

BINDER	WRAPPER

APPEARANCE

CONSTRUCTION

DRAW	START	1/2	3/4
BURN	START	1/2	3/4

TASTING NOTES

OTHER NOTES

EVALUATION

O O O O O O O O O O

POOR   CLASSIC

RECOMMEND AND ENJOY AGAIN?   Y   N

Cigar Log Entry

MINUTIAE	DATE		OCCASION		
BRAND				PRICE	
VITOLA	GAUGE		LENGTH		
SHAPE NAME					
ANATOMY	FILLER				
BINDER			WRAPPER		
APPEARANCE					
CONSTRUCTION					
DRAW	START		1/2		3/4
BURN	START		1/2		3/4

TASTING NOTES

OTHER NOTES

EVALUATION

O O O O O O O O O O

POOR   CLASSIC

RECOMMEND AND ENJOY AGAIN?   Y   N

ATTACH BAND HERE

Cigar Log Entry

ATTACH BAND HERE

MINUTIAE	DATE	OCCASION	
BRAND			PRICE
VITOLA	GAUGE	LENGTH	
SHAPE NAME			
ANATOMY	FILLER		
BINDER		WRAPPER	
APPEARANCE			

CONSTRUCTION

DRAW	START	1/2	3/4
BURN	START	1/2	3/4

TASTING NOTES

OTHER NOTES

EVALUATION

O   O   O   O   O   O   O   O   O   O

POOR   CLASSIC

RECOMMEND AND ENJOY AGAIN?   Y   N

Cigar Log Entry

MINUTIAE	DATE	OCCASION	
BRAND			PRICE
VITOLA	GAUGE	LENGTH	
SHAPE NAME			
ANATOMY	FILLER		
BINDER		WRAPPER	

APPEARANCE

CONSTRUCTION

DRAW	START	1/2	3/4
BURN	START	1/2	3/4

TASTING NOTES

OTHER NOTES

EVALUATION

○ ○ ○ ○ ○ ○ ○ ○ ○ ○

POOR · · · · · · · · · · CLASSIC

RECOMMEND AND ENJOY AGAIN? Y N

ATTACH BAND HERE

Cigar Log Entry

ATTACH BAND HERE

MINUTIAE	DATE		OCCASION		
BRAND					PRICE
VITOLA	GAUGE		LENGTH		
SHAPE NAME					
ANATOMY	FILLER				
BINDER			WRAPPER		
APPEARANCE					
CONSTRUCTION					

DRAW	START	1/2	3/4
BURN	START	1/2	3/4

TASTING NOTES

OTHER NOTES

EVALUATION

○ ○ ○ ○ ○ ○ ○ ○ ○ ○

POOR   CLASSIC

RECOMMEND AND ENJOY AGAIN?   Y   N

Cigar Log Entry

MINUTIAE	DATE	OCCASION	

BRAND			PRICE

VITOLA	GAUGE		LENGTH

SHAPE NAME			

ANATOMY	FILLER		

BINDER		WRAPPER	

APPEARANCE

CONSTRUCTION

DRAW	START	1/2	3/4
BURN	START	1/2	3/4

TASTING NOTES

OTHER NOTES

EVALUATION

O O O O O O O O O O

POOR   CLASSIC

RECOMMEND AND ENJOY AGAIN?   Y   N

ATTACH BAND HERE

Cigar Log Entry

ATTACH BAND HERE

MINUTIAE	DATE		OCCASION		
BRAND					PRICE
VITOLA	GAUGE		LENGTH		
SHAPE NAME					
ANATOMY	FILLER				
BINDER			WRAPPER		

APPEARANCE

CONSTRUCTION

DRAW	START		1/2		3/4
BURN	START		1/2		3/4

TASTING NOTES

OTHER NOTES

EVALUATION

O O O O O O O O O O

POOR   CLASSIC

RECOMMEND AND ENJOY AGAIN?   Y   N

Cigar Log Entry

MINUTIAE	DATE		OCCASION		
BRAND					PRICE
VITOLA	GAUGE		LENGTH		
SHAPE NAME					
ANATOMY	FILLER				
BINDER			WRAPPER		

APPEARANCE

CONSTRUCTION

DRAW	START	1/2	3/4
BURN	START	1/2	3/4

TASTING NOTES

OTHER NOTES

EVALUATION

O O O O O O O O O O

POOR   CLASSIC

RECOMMEND AND ENJOY AGAIN?   Y   N

ATTACH BAND HERE

Cigar Log Entry

ATTACH BAND HERE

MINUTIAE	DATE	OCCASION	
BRAND			PRICE
VITOLA	GAUGE	LENGTH	
SHAPE NAME			
ANATOMY	FILLER		
BINDER		WRAPPER	
APPEARANCE			

CONSTRUCTION

DRAW	START	1/2	3/4
BURN	START	1/2	3/4

TASTING NOTES

OTHER NOTES

EVALUATION

○ ○ ○ ○ ○ ○ ○ ○ ○ ○

POOR   CLASSIC

RECOMMEND AND ENJOY AGAIN?   Y   N

Cigar Log Entry

MINUTIAE	DATE	OCCASION	

BRAND			PRICE

VITOLA	GAUGE		LENGTH

SHAPE NAME

ANATOMY	FILLER

BINDER		WRAPPER

APPEARANCE

CONSTRUCTION

DRAW	START	1/2	3/4
BURN	START	1/2	3/4

TASTING NOTES

OTHER NOTES

EVALUATION

O O O O O O O O O O

POOR   CLASSIC

RECOMMEND AND ENJOY AGAIN?   Y   N

ATTACH BAND HERE

Cigar Log Entry

ATTACH BAND HERE

MINUTIAE	DATE		OCCASION		
BRAND					PRICE
VITOLA	GAUGE		LENGTH		
SHAPE NAME					
ANATOMY	FILLER				
BINDER			WRAPPER		
APPEARANCE					
CONSTRUCTION					

DRAW	START	1/2	3/4
BURN	START	1/2	3/4

TASTING NOTES

OTHER NOTES

EVALUATION

O O O O O O O O O O

POOR　　　　　　　　　　　　　　　　CLASSIC

RECOMMEND AND ENJOY AGAIN?　　Y　　N

Cigar Log Entry

MINUTIAE	DATE		OCCASION		
BRAND				PRICE	
VITOLA	GAUGE		LENGTH		
SHAPE NAME					
ANATOMY	FILLER				
BINDER			WRAPPER		
APPEARANCE					
CONSTRUCTION					
DRAW	START	1/2		3/4	
BURN	START	1/2		3/4	

TASTING NOTES

OTHER NOTES

EVALUATION

O O O O O O O O O O

POOR   CLASSIC

RECOMMEND AND ENJOY AGAIN?   Y   N

ATTACH BAND HERE

Cigar Log Entry

ATTACH BAND HERE

MINUTIAE	DATE	OCCASION	
BRAND			PRICE
VITOLA	GAUGE	LENGTH	
SHAPE NAME			
ANATOMY	FILLER		
BINDER		WRAPPER	
APPEARANCE			

CONSTRUCTION

DRAW	START	1/2	3/4
BURN	START	1/2	3/4

TASTING NOTES

OTHER NOTES

EVALUATION

O O O O O O O O O O

POOR CLASSIC

RECOMMEND AND ENJOY AGAIN?   Y   N

Cigar Log Entry

MINUTIAE	DATE		OCCASION		
BRAND					PRICE
VITOLA	GAUGE			LENGTH	
SHAPE NAME					
ANATOMY	FILLER				
BINDER			WRAPPER		

APPEARANCE

CONSTRUCTION

DRAW	START	1/2	3/4
BURN	START	1/2	3/4

TASTING NOTES

OTHER NOTES

EVALUATION

○ ○ ○ ○ ○ ○ ○ ○ ○ ○

POOR   CLASSIC

RECOMMEND AND ENJOY AGAIN?   Y   N

ATTACH BAND HERE

Cigar Log Entry

ATTACH BAND HERE

MINUTIAE	DATE	OCCASION	

BRAND		PRICE

VITOLA	GAUGE	LENGTH

SHAPE NAME

ANATOMY	FILLER

BINDER	WRAPPER

APPEARANCE

CONSTRUCTION

DRAW	START	1/2	3/4
BURN	START	1/2	3/4

TASTING NOTES

OTHER NOTES

EVALUATION

◯ ◯ ◯ ◯ ◯ ◯ ◯ ◯ ◯ ◯

POOR   CLASSIC

RECOMMEND AND ENJOY AGAIN?   Y   N

Cigar Log Entry

MINUTIAE	DATE	OCCASION	
BRAND			PRICE
VITOLA	GAUGE		LENGTH
SHAPE NAME			
ANATOMY	FILLER		
BINDER		WRAPPER	

APPEARANCE

CONSTRUCTION

DRAW	START	1/2	3/4
BURN	START	1/2	3/4

TASTING NOTES

OTHER NOTES

EVALUATION

◯ ◯ ◯ ◯ ◯ ◯ ◯ ◯ ◯ ◯

POOR   CLASSIC

RECOMMEND AND ENJOY AGAIN?   Y   N

ATTACH BAND HERE

Cigar Log Entry

ATTACH BAND HERE

MINUTIAE	DATE	OCCASION	

BRAND			PRICE

VITOLA	GAUGE		LENGTH

SHAPE NAME

ANATOMY	FILLER

BINDER		WRAPPER

APPEARANCE

CONSTRUCTION

DRAW	START	1/2	3/4
BURN	START	1/2	3/4

TASTING NOTES

OTHER NOTES

EVALUATION

○ ○ ○ ○ ○ ○ ○ ○ ○ ○

POOR   CLASSIC

RECOMMEND AND ENJOY AGAIN?   Y   N

Cigar Log Entry

MINUTIAE	DATE	OCCASION		
BRAND				PRICE
VITOLA	GAUGE		LENGTH	
SHAPE NAME				
ANATOMY	FILLER			
BINDER			WRAPPER	

APPEARANCE

CONSTRUCTION

DRAW	START	1/2	3/4
BURN	START	1/2	3/4

TASTING NOTES

OTHER NOTES

EVALUATION

O O O O O O O O O O

POOR   CLASSIC

RECOMMEND AND ENJOY AGAIN?   Y   N

ATTACH BAND HERE

Cigar Log Entry

ATTACH BAND HERE

MINUTIAE	DATE	OCCASION	

BRAND		PRICE

VITOLA	GAUGE	LENGTH	

SHAPE NAME

ANATOMY	FILLER

BINDER	WRAPPER

APPEARANCE

CONSTRUCTION

DRAW	START	1/2	3/4
BURN	START	1/2	3/4

TASTING NOTES

OTHER NOTES

EVALUATION

O O O O O O O O O O

POOR   CLASSIC

RECOMMEND AND ENJOY AGAIN?   Y   N

Cigar Log Entry

MINUTIAE	DATE	OCCASION	
BRAND			PRICE
VITOLA	GAUGE		LENGTH
SHAPE NAME			
ANATOMY	FILLER		
BINDER		WRAPPER	

APPEARANCE

CONSTRUCTION

DRAW	START	1/2	3/4
BURN	START	1/2	3/4

TASTING NOTES

OTHER NOTES

EVALUATION

○ ○ ○ ○ ○ ○ ○ ○ ○ ○

POOR   CLASSIC

RECOMMEND AND ENJOY AGAIN?   Y   N

ATTACH BAND HERE

Cigar Log Entry

```
ATTACH BAND HERE
```

MINUTIAE	DATE		OCCASION		
BRAND				PRICE	
VITOLA	GAUGE		LENGTH		
SHAPE NAME					
ANATOMY	FILLER				
BINDER			WRAPPER		
APPEARANCE					
CONSTRUCTION					
DRAW	START	1/2		3/4	
BURN	START	1/2		3/4	

TASTING NOTES

OTHER NOTES

EVALUATION

○ ○ ○ ○ ○ ○ ○ ○ ○ ○

POOR   CLASSIC

RECOMMEND AND ENJOY AGAIN?   Y   N

Cigar Log Entry

MINUTIAE	DATE	OCCASION	
BRAND			PRICE
VITOLA	GAUGE		LENGTH
SHAPE NAME			
ANATOMY	FILLER		
BINDER		WRAPPER	
APPEARANCE			
CONSTRUCTION			

DRAW	START	1/2	3/4
BURN	START	1/2	3/4

TASTING NOTES

OTHER NOTES

EVALUATION

O O O O O O O O O O

POOR   CLASSIC

RECOMMEND AND ENJOY AGAIN?   Y   N

ATTACH BAND HERE

Cigar Log Entry

ATTACH BAND HERE

MINUTIAE	DATE	OCCASION	

BRAND			PRICE

VITOLA	GAUGE		LENGTH

SHAPE NAME

ANATOMY	FILLER

BINDER	WRAPPER

APPEARANCE

CONSTRUCTION

DRAW	START	1/2	3/4
BURN	START	1/2	3/4

TASTING NOTES

OTHER NOTES

EVALUATION

O O O O O O O O O O

POOR   CLASSIC

RECOMMEND AND ENJOY AGAIN?   Y   N

Cigar Log Entry

MINUTIAE	DATE		OCCASION		
BRAND					PRICE
VITOLA	GAUGE			LENGTH	
SHAPE NAME					
ANATOMY	FILLER				
BINDER			WRAPPER		

APPEARANCE

CONSTRUCTION

DRAW	START		1/2		3/4
BURN	START		1/2		3/4

TASTING NOTES

OTHER NOTES

EVALUATION

O O O O O O O O O O

POOR   CLASSIC

RECOMMEND AND ENJOY AGAIN?   Y   N

ATTACH BAND HERE

Cigar Log Entry

ATTACH BAND HERE

MINUTIAE	DATE	OCCASION		
BRAND			PRICE	
VITOLA	GAUGE	LENGTH		
SHAPE NAME				
ANATOMY	FILLER			
BINDER		WRAPPER		
APPEARANCE				

CONSTRUCTION

DRAW	START	1/2	3/4
BURN	START	1/2	3/4

TASTING NOTES

OTHER NOTES

EVALUATION

O O O O O O O O O O

POOR   CLASSIC

RECOMMEND AND ENJOY AGAIN?   Y   N

Cigar Log Entry

MINUTIAE	DATE		OCCASION		
BRAND					PRICE
VITOLA	GAUGE		LENGTH		
SHAPE NAME					
ANATOMY	FILLER				
BINDER			WRAPPER		

APPEARANCE

CONSTRUCTION

DRAW	START	1/2	3/4
BURN	START	1/2	3/4

TASTING NOTES

OTHER NOTES

EVALUATION

O O O O O O O O O O

POOR   CLASSIC

RECOMMEND AND ENJOY AGAIN?   Y   N

ATTACH BAND HERE

Cigar Log Entry

ATTACH BAND HERE

MINUTIAE	DATE	OCCASION	

BRAND			PRICE

VITOLA	GAUGE	LENGTH	

SHAPE NAME

ANATOMY	FILLER	

BINDER		WRAPPER

APPEARANCE

CONSTRUCTION

DRAW	START	1/2	3/4
BURN	START	1/2	3/4

TASTING NOTES

OTHER NOTES

EVALUATION

O O O O O O O O O O

POOR   CLASSIC

RECOMMEND AND ENJOY AGAIN?   Y   N

Cigar Log Entry

MINUTIAE	DATE	OCCASION		
BRAND				PRICE
VITOLA	GAUGE		LENGTH	
SHAPE NAME				
ANATOMY	FILLER			
BINDER		WRAPPER		
APPEARANCE				
CONSTRUCTION				

DRAW	START	1/2	3/4
BURN	START	1/2	3/4

TASTING NOTES

OTHER NOTES

EVALUATION

O O O O O O O O O O

POOR CLASSIC

RECOMMEND AND ENJOY AGAIN? Y N

ATTACH BAND HERE

Cigar Log Entry

ATTACH BAND HERE

MINUTIAE	DATE		OCCASION		
BRAND					PRICE
VITOLA	GAUGE		LENGTH		
SHAPE NAME					
ANATOMY	FILLER				
BINDER			WRAPPER		
APPEARANCE					
CONSTRUCTION					
DRAW	START	1/2		3/4	
BURN	START	1/2		3/4	

TASTING NOTES

OTHER NOTES

EVALUATION

O O O O O O O O O O

POOR   CLASSIC

RECOMMEND AND ENJOY AGAIN?   Y   N

Cigar Log Entry

MINUTIAE	DATE	OCCASION	
BRAND			PRICE
VITOLA	GAUGE		LENGTH
SHAPE NAME			
ANATOMY	FILLER		
BINDER		WRAPPER	

APPEARANCE

CONSTRUCTION

DRAW	START	1/2	3/4
BURN	START	1/2	3/4

TASTING NOTES

OTHER NOTES

EVALUATION

○ ○ ○ ○ ○ ○ ○ ○ ○ ○

POOR   CLASSIC

RECOMMEND AND ENJOY AGAIN?   Y   N

ATTACH BAND HERE

Cigar Log Entry

ATTACH BAND HERE

MINUTIAE	DATE	OCCASION	

BRAND		PRICE

VITOLA	GAUGE	LENGTH

SHAPE NAME

ANATOMY	FILLER

BINDER	WRAPPER

APPEARANCE

CONSTRUCTION

DRAW	START	1/2	3/4
BURN	START	1/2	3/4

TASTING NOTES

OTHER NOTES

EVALUATION

◯ ◯ ◯ ◯ ◯ ◯ ◯ ◯ ◯ ◯

POOR   CLASSIC

RECOMMEND AND ENJOY AGAIN?   Y   N

Cigar Log Entry

MINUTIAE	DATE		OCCASION		
BRAND					PRICE
VITOLA	GAUGE			LENGTH	
SHAPE NAME					
ANATOMY	FILLER				
BINDER				WRAPPER	
APPEARANCE					
CONSTRUCTION					

DRAW	START	1/2	3/4
BURN	START	1/2	3/4

TASTING NOTES

OTHER NOTES

EVALUATION

O O O O O O O O O O

POOR   CLASSIC

RECOMMEND AND ENJOY AGAIN?   Y   N

ATTACH BAND HERE

Cigar Log Entry

ATTACH BAND HERE

MINUTIAE	DATE	OCCASION	

BRAND		PRICE

VITOLA	GAUGE	LENGTH	

SHAPE NAME

ANATOMY	FILLER

BINDER	WRAPPER

APPEARANCE

CONSTRUCTION

DRAW	START	1/2	3/4
BURN	START	1/2	3/4

TASTING NOTES

OTHER NOTES

EVALUATION

O O O O O O O O O O

POOR　　　　　　　　　　　　　　　　CLASSIC

RECOMMEND AND ENJOY AGAIN?　　Y　　N

Cigar Log Entry

MINUTIAE	DATE		OCCASION		
BRAND					PRICE
VITOLA	GAUGE		LENGTH		
SHAPE NAME					
ANATOMY	FILLER				
BINDER			WRAPPER		

APPEARANCE

CONSTRUCTION

DRAW	START	1/2	3/4
BURN	START	1/2	3/4

TASTING NOTES

OTHER NOTES

EVALUATION

O O O O O O O O O O

POOR   CLASSIC

RECOMMEND AND ENJOY AGAIN?   Y   N

ATTACH BAND HERE

Cigar Log Entry

ATTACH BAND HERE

MINUTIAE	DATE		OCCASION		
BRAND					PRICE
VITOLA	GAUGE			LENGTH	
SHAPE NAME					
ANATOMY	FILLER				
BINDER			WRAPPER		
APPEARANCE					

CONSTRUCTION

DRAW	START	1/2	3/4
BURN	START	1/2	3/4

TASTING NOTES

OTHER NOTES

EVALUATION

O O O O O O O O O O

POOR   CLASSIC

RECOMMEND AND ENJOY AGAIN?   Y   N

Cigar Log Entry

MINUTIAE	DATE	OCCASION	

BRAND			PRICE

VITOLA	GAUGE		LENGTH	

SHAPE NAME

ANATOMY	FILLER

BINDER		WRAPPER

APPEARANCE

CONSTRUCTION

DRAW	START	1/2	3/4
BURN	START	1/2	3/4

TASTING NOTES

OTHER NOTES

EVALUATION

○ ○ ○ ○ ○ ○ ○ ○ ○ ○

POOR   CLASSIC

RECOMMEND AND ENJOY AGAIN?   Y   N

ATTACH BAND HERE

Cigar Log Entry

ATTACH BAND HERE

MINUTIAE	DATE		OCCASION		
BRAND				PRICE	
VITOLA	GAUGE		LENGTH		
SHAPE NAME					
ANATOMY	FILLER				
BINDER			WRAPPER		
APPEARANCE					

CONSTRUCTION

DRAW	START	1/2	3/4
BURN	START	1/2	3/4

TASTING NOTES

OTHER NOTES

EVALUATION

○ ○ ○ ○ ○ ○ ○ ○ ○ ○

POOR   CLASSIC

RECOMMEND AND ENJOY AGAIN?   Y   N

Cigar Log Entry

MINUTIAE	DATE		OCCASION		
BRAND					PRICE
VITOLA	GAUGE		LENGTH		
SHAPE NAME					
ANATOMY	FILLER				
BINDER			WRAPPER		

APPEARANCE

CONSTRUCTION

DRAW	START	1/2	3/4
BURN	START	1/2	3/4

TASTING NOTES

OTHER NOTES

EVALUATION

O O O O O O O O O O

POOR   CLASSIC

RECOMMEND AND ENJOY AGAIN?   Y   N

ATTACH BAND HERE

Cigar Log Entry

ATTACH BAND HERE

MINUTIAE	DATE		OCCASION		
BRAND					PRICE
VITOLA	GAUGE		LENGTH		
SHAPE NAME					
ANATOMY	FILLER				
BINDER			WRAPPER		
APPEARANCE					

CONSTRUCTION

DRAW	START	1/2	3/4
BURN	START	1/2	3/4

TASTING NOTES

OTHER NOTES

EVALUATION

O O O O O O O O O O

POOR   CLASSIC

RECOMMEND AND ENJOY AGAIN?   Y   N

Cigar Log Entry

MINUTIAE	DATE	OCCASION	
BRAND			PRICE
VITOLA	GAUGE	LENGTH	
SHAPE NAME			
ANATOMY	FILLER		
BINDER		WRAPPER	
APPEARANCE			

CONSTRUCTION

DRAW	START	1/2	3/4
BURN	START	1/2	3/4

TASTING NOTES

OTHER NOTES

EVALUATION

O O O O O O O O O O

POOR   CLASSIC

RECOMMEND AND ENJOY AGAIN?   Y   N

ATTACH BAND HERE

Cigar Log Entry

ATTACH BAND HERE

MINUTIAE	DATE	OCCASION	
BRAND			PRICE
VITOLA	GAUGE	LENGTH	
SHAPE NAME			
ANATOMY	FILLER		
BINDER		WRAPPER	
APPEARANCE			

CONSTRUCTION			

DRAW	START	1/2	3/4
BURN	START	1/2	3/4

TASTING NOTES

OTHER NOTES

EVALUATION

○ ○ ○ ○ ○ ○ ○ ○ ○ ○

POOR   CLASSIC

RECOMMEND AND ENJOY AGAIN?   Y   N

Cigar Log Entry

MINUTIAE	DATE	OCCASION	
BRAND			PRICE
VITOLA	GAUGE	LENGTH	
SHAPE NAME			
ANATOMY	FILLER		
BINDER		WRAPPER	
APPEARANCE			
CONSTRUCTION			

DRAW	START	1/2	3/4
BURN	START	1/2	3/4

TASTING NOTES

OTHER NOTES

EVALUATION

O O O O O O O O O O

POOR   CLASSIC

RECOMMEND AND ENJOY AGAIN?   Y   N

ATTACH BAND HERE

Cigar Log Entry

ATTACH BAND HERE

MINUTIAE	DATE	OCCASION	

BRAND			PRICE

VITOLA	GAUGE		LENGTH

SHAPE NAME

ANATOMY	FILLER

BINDER		WRAPPER

APPEARANCE

CONSTRUCTION

DRAW	START	1/2	3/4
BURN	START	1/2	3/4

TASTING NOTES

OTHER NOTES

EVALUATION

O O O O O O O O O O

POOR   CLASSIC

RECOMMEND AND ENJOY AGAIN?   Y   N

Cigar Log Entry

MINUTIAE	DATE		OCCASION		
BRAND				PRICE	
VITOLA	GAUGE		LENGTH		
SHAPE NAME					
ANATOMY	FILLER				
BINDER			WRAPPER		
APPEARANCE					
CONSTRUCTION					

DRAW	START	1/2	3/4
BURN	START	1/2	3/4

TASTING NOTES

OTHER NOTES

EVALUATION

⭘ ⭘ ⭘ ⭘ ⭘ ⭘ ⭘ ⭘ ⭘ ⭘

POOR   CLASSIC

RECOMMEND AND ENJOY AGAIN?   Y   N

ATTACH BAND HERE

Cigar Log Entry

ATTACH BAND HERE

MINUTIAE	DATE		OCCASION		
BRAND					PRICE
VITOLA	GAUGE		LENGTH		
SHAPE NAME					
ANATOMY	FILLER				
BINDER			WRAPPER		
APPEARANCE					
CONSTRUCTION					
DRAW	START	1/2		3/4	
BURN	START	1/2		3/4	

TASTING NOTES

OTHER NOTES

EVALUATION

○ ○ ○ ○ ○ ○ ○ ○ ○ ○

POOR   CLASSIC

RECOMMEND AND ENJOY AGAIN?   Y   N

Cigar Log Entry

MINUTIAE	DATE		OCCASION	
BRAND				PRICE
VITOLA	GAUGE		LENGTH	
SHAPE NAME				
ANATOMY	FILLER			
BINDER			WRAPPER	

APPEARANCE

CONSTRUCTION

DRAW	START	1/2	3/4
BURN	START	1/2	3/4

TASTING NOTES

OTHER NOTES

EVALUATION

O O O O O O O O O O

POOR   CLASSIC

RECOMMEND AND ENJOY AGAIN?   Y   N

ATTACH BAND HERE

Cigar Log Entry

ATTACH BAND HERE

MINUTIAE	DATE		OCCASION		
BRAND					PRICE
VITOLA	GAUGE		LENGTH		
SHAPE NAME					
ANATOMY	FILLER				
BINDER			WRAPPER		
APPEARANCE					

CONSTRUCTION

DRAW	START	1/2	3/4
BURN	START	1/2	3/4

TASTING NOTES

OTHER NOTES

EVALUATION

○ ○ ○ ○ ○ ○ ○ ○ ○ ○

POOR   CLASSIC

RECOMMEND AND ENJOY AGAIN?   Y   N

Cigar Log Entry

MINUTIAE	DATE	OCCASION	
BRAND			PRICE
VITOLA	GAUGE	LENGTH	
SHAPE NAME			
ANATOMY	FILLER		
BINDER		WRAPPER	
APPEARANCE			
CONSTRUCTION			

DRAW	START	1/2	3/4
BURN	START	1/2	3/4

TASTING NOTES

OTHER NOTES

EVALUATION

○ ○ ○ ○ ○ ○ ○ ○ ○ ○

POOR   CLASSIC

RECOMMEND AND ENJOY AGAIN?   **Y**   **N**

ATTACH BAND HERE

Cigar Log Entry

ATTACH BAND HERE

MINUTIAE	DATE	OCCASION	

BRAND			PRICE

VITOLA	GAUGE	LENGTH	

SHAPE NAME			

ANATOMY	FILLER		

BINDER		WRAPPER	

APPEARANCE

CONSTRUCTION

DRAW	START	1/2	3/4
BURN	START	1/2	3/4

TASTING NOTES

OTHER NOTES

EVALUATION

○ ○ ○ ○ ○ ○ ○ ○ ○ ○

POOR   CLASSIC

RECOMMEND AND ENJOY AGAIN?   Y   N

Cigar Log Entry

MINUTIAE	DATE		OCCASION		
BRAND				PRICE	
VITOLA	GAUGE		LENGTH		
SHAPE NAME					
ANATOMY	FILLER				
BINDER			WRAPPER		
APPEARANCE					
CONSTRUCTION					

DRAW	START	1/2	3/4
BURN	START	1/2	3/4

TASTING NOTES

OTHER NOTES

EVALUATION

○ ○ ○ ○ ○ ○ ○ ○ ○ ○

POOR   CLASSIC

RECOMMEND AND ENJOY AGAIN?   **Y**   **N**

ATTACH BAND HERE

Cigar Log Entry

ATTACH BAND HERE

MINUTIAE	DATE		OCCASION		
BRAND				PRICE	
VITOLA	GAUGE		LENGTH		
SHAPE NAME					
ANATOMY	FILLER				
BINDER			WRAPPER		
APPEARANCE					

CONSTRUCTION

DRAW	START	1/2	3/4
BURN	START	1/2	3/4

TASTING NOTES

OTHER NOTES

EVALUATION

O O O O O O O O O O

POOR   CLASSIC

RECOMMEND AND ENJOY AGAIN?   Y   N

Cigar Log Entry

MINUTIAE	DATE	OCCASION	
BRAND			PRICE
VITOLA	GAUGE	LENGTH	
SHAPE NAME			
ANATOMY	FILLER		
BINDER		WRAPPER	

APPEARANCE

CONSTRUCTION

DRAW	START	1/2	3/4
BURN	START	1/2	3/4

TASTING NOTES

OTHER NOTES

EVALUATION

O O O O O O O O O O

POOR   CLASSIC

RECOMMEND AND ENJOY AGAIN?   Y   N

ATTACH BAND HERE

Cigar Log Entry

ATTACH BAND HERE

MINUTIAE	DATE	OCCASION	
BRAND			PRICE
VITOLA	GAUGE	LENGTH	
SHAPE NAME			
ANATOMY	FILLER		
BINDER		WRAPPER	
APPEARANCE			
CONSTRUCTION			
DRAW	START	1/2	3/4
BURN	START	1/2	3/4

TASTING NOTES

OTHER NOTES

EVALUATION

O O O O O O O O O O

POOR   CLASSIC

RECOMMEND AND ENJOY AGAIN?   Y   N

Cigar Log Entry

MINUTIAE	DATE		OCCASION		
BRAND					PRICE
VITOLA	GAUGE			LENGTH	
SHAPE NAME					
ANATOMY	FILLER				
BINDER				WRAPPER	
APPEARANCE					
CONSTRUCTION					

DRAW	START	1/2	3/4
BURN	START	1/2	3/4

TASTING NOTES

OTHER NOTES

EVALUATION

O O O O O O O O O O

POOR   CLASSIC

RECOMMEND AND ENJOY AGAIN?   Y   N

ATTACH BAND HERE

Cigar Log Entry

ATTACH BAND HERE

MINUTIAE	DATE		OCCASION		
BRAND				PRICE	
VITOLA	GAUGE		LENGTH		
SHAPE NAME					
ANATOMY	FILLER				
BINDER			WRAPPER		
APPEARANCE					
CONSTRUCTION					
DRAW	START	1/2		3/4	
BURN	START	1/2		3/4	

TASTING NOTES

OTHER NOTES

EVALUATION

O O O O O O O O O O

POOR   CLASSIC

RECOMMEND AND ENJOY AGAIN?   Y   N

Cigar Log Entry

MINUTIAE	DATE	OCCASION	

BRAND			PRICE

VITOLA	GAUGE	LENGTH	

SHAPE NAME			

ANATOMY	FILLER		

BINDER		WRAPPER	

APPEARANCE

CONSTRUCTION

DRAW	START	1/2	3/4
BURN	START	1/2	3/4

TASTING NOTES

OTHER NOTES

EVALUATION

O   O   O   O   O   O   O   O   O   O

POOR   CLASSIC

RECOMMEND AND ENJOY AGAIN?   Y   N

ATTACH BAND HERE

Cigar Log Entry

ATTACH BAND HERE

MINUTIAE	DATE		OCCASION		
BRAND				PRICE	
VITOLA	GAUGE		LENGTH		
SHAPE NAME					
ANATOMY	FILLER				
BINDER			WRAPPER		
APPEARANCE					

CONSTRUCTION

DRAW	START	1/2	3/4
BURN	START	1/2	3/4

TASTING NOTES

OTHER NOTES

EVALUATION

○ ○ ○ ○ ○ ○ ○ ○ ○ ○

POOR   CLASSIC

RECOMMEND AND ENJOY AGAIN?   Y   N

Cigar Log Entry

MINUTIAE	DATE	OCCASION		
BRAND				PRICE
VITOLA	GAUGE		LENGTH	
SHAPE NAME				
ANATOMY	FILLER			
BINDER		WRAPPER		

APPEARANCE

CONSTRUCTION

DRAW	START	1/2	3/4
BURN	START	1/2	3/4

TASTING NOTES

OTHER NOTES

EVALUATION

O O O O O O O O O O

POOR   CLASSIC

RECOMMEND AND ENJOY AGAIN?   Y   N

ATTACH BAND HERE

Cigar Log Entry

ATTACH BAND HERE

MINUTIAE	DATE		OCCASION	
BRAND				PRICE
VITOLA	GAUGE		LENGTH	
SHAPE NAME				
ANATOMY	FILLER			
BINDER			WRAPPER	
APPEARANCE				
CONSTRUCTION				
DRAW	START	1/2		3/4
BURN	START	1/2		3/4
TASTING NOTES				
OTHER NOTES				
EVALUATION				

EVALUATION

○ ○ ○ ○ ○ ○ ○ ○ ○ ○

POOR   CLASSIC

RECOMMEND AND ENJOY AGAIN?   Y   N

Cigar Log Entry

MINUTIAE	DATE		OCCASION		
BRAND					PRICE
VITOLA	GAUGE			LENGTH	
SHAPE NAME					
ANATOMY	FILLER				
BINDER				WRAPPER	

APPEARANCE

CONSTRUCTION

DRAW	START	1/2	3/4
BURN	START	1/2	3/4

TASTING NOTES

OTHER NOTES

EVALUATION

○ ○ ○ ○ ○ ○ ○ ○ ○ ○

POOR   CLASSIC

RECOMMEND AND ENJOY AGAIN?   Y   N

ATTACH BAND HERE

Cigar Log Entry

ATTACH BAND HERE

MINUTIAE	DATE		OCCASION		

BRAND				PRICE	

VITOLA	GAUGE		LENGTH	

SHAPE NAME

ANATOMY	FILLER

BINDER		WRAPPER	

APPEARANCE

CONSTRUCTION

DRAW	START		1/2		3/4	
BURN	START		1/2		3/4	

TASTING NOTES

OTHER NOTES

EVALUATION

O O O O O O O O O O

POOR   CLASSIC

RECOMMEND AND ENJOY AGAIN?   Y   N

Cigar Log Entry

MINUTIAE	DATE		OCCASION		
BRAND					PRICE
VITOLA	GAUGE		LENGTH		
SHAPE NAME					
ANATOMY	FILLER				
BINDER			WRAPPER		

APPEARANCE

CONSTRUCTION

DRAW	START	1/2	3/4
BURN	START	1/2	3/4

TASTING NOTES

OTHER NOTES

EVALUATION

O O O O O O O O O O

POOR   CLASSIC

RECOMMEND AND ENJOY AGAIN?   Y   N

ATTACH BAND HERE

Cigar Log Entry

ATTACH BAND HERE

MINUTIAE	DATE		OCCASION	
BRAND				PRICE
VITOLA	GAUGE		LENGTH	
SHAPE NAME				
ANATOMY	FILLER			
BINDER			WRAPPER	
APPEARANCE				

CONSTRUCTION

DRAW	START	1/2	3/4
BURN	START	1/2	3/4

TASTING NOTES

OTHER NOTES

EVALUATION

O   O   O   O   O   O   O   O   O   O

POOR   CLASSIC

RECOMMEND AND ENJOY AGAIN?   Y   N

Cigar Log Entry

MINUTIAE	DATE	OCCASION		
BRAND				PRICE
VITOLA	GAUGE		LENGTH	
SHAPE NAME				
ANATOMY	FILLER			
BINDER			WRAPPER	

APPEARANCE

CONSTRUCTION

DRAW	START	1/2	3/4
BURN	START	1/2	3/4

TASTING NOTES

OTHER NOTES

EVALUATION

O O O O O O O O O O

POOR   CLASSIC

RECOMMEND AND ENJOY AGAIN?   Y   N

ATTACH BAND HERE

Cigar Log Entry

ATTACH BAND HERE

MINUTIAE	DATE	OCCASION	

BRAND			PRICE

VITOLA	GAUGE		LENGTH

SHAPE NAME			

ANATOMY	FILLER		

BINDER		WRAPPER	

APPEARANCE

CONSTRUCTION

DRAW	START	1/2	3/4
BURN	START	1/2	3/4

TASTING NOTES

OTHER NOTES

EVALUATION

O O O O O O O O O O

POOR   CLASSIC

RECOMMEND AND ENJOY AGAIN?   Y   N

Cigar Log Entry

MINUTIAE	DATE	OCCASION	
BRAND			PRICE
VITOLA	GAUGE	LENGTH	
SHAPE NAME			
ANATOMY	FILLER		
BINDER		WRAPPER	
APPEARANCE			
CONSTRUCTION			

DRAW	START	1/2	3/4
BURN	START	1/2	3/4

TASTING NOTES

OTHER NOTES

EVALUATION

O O O O O O O O O O

POOR   CLASSIC

RECOMMEND AND ENJOY AGAIN?   Y   N

ATTACH BAND HERE

Cigar Log Entry

ATTACH BAND HERE

MINUTIAE	DATE		OCCASION	
BRAND				PRICE
VITOLA	GAUGE		LENGTH	
SHAPE NAME				
ANATOMY	FILLER			
BINDER			WRAPPER	
APPEARANCE				
CONSTRUCTION				

DRAW	START	1/2	3/4
BURN	START	1/2	3/4

TASTING NOTES

OTHER NOTES

EVALUATION

○ ○ ○ ○ ○ ○ ○ ○ ○ ○

POOR   CLASSIC

RECOMMEND AND ENJOY AGAIN?   Y   N

Cigar Log Entry

MINUTIAE	DATE	OCCASION	
BRAND			PRICE
VITOLA	GAUGE	LENGTH	
SHAPE NAME			
ANATOMY	FILLER		
BINDER		WRAPPER	

APPEARANCE

CONSTRUCTION

DRAW	START	1/2	3/4
BURN	START	1/2	3/4

TASTING NOTES

OTHER NOTES

EVALUATION

O O O O O O O O O O

POOR   CLASSIC

RECOMMEND AND ENJOY AGAIN?   Y   N

ATTACH BAND HERE

Cigar Log Entry

ATTACH BAND HERE

MINUTIAE	DATE	OCCASION	

BRAND		PRICE

VITOLA	GAUGE	LENGTH	

SHAPE NAME

ANATOMY	FILLER

BINDER	WRAPPER

APPEARANCE

CONSTRUCTION

DRAW	START	1/2	3/4
BURN	START	1/2	3/4

TASTING NOTES

OTHER NOTES

EVALUATION

O O O O O O O O O O

POOR   CLASSIC

RECOMMEND AND ENJOY AGAIN?   Y   N

Cigar Log Entry

MINUTIAE	DATE	OCCASION	
BRAND			PRICE
VITOLA	GAUGE		LENGTH
SHAPE NAME			
ANATOMY	FILLER		
BINDER		WRAPPER	
APPEARANCE			
CONSTRUCTION			

DRAW	START	1/2	3/4
BURN	START	1/2	3/4

TASTING NOTES

OTHER NOTES

EVALUATION

O O O O O O O O O O

POOR   CLASSIC

RECOMMEND AND ENJOY AGAIN?   Y   N

ATTACH BAND HERE

Cigar Log Entry

ATTACH BAND HERE

MINUTIAE	DATE	OCCASION	
BRAND			PRICE
VITOLA	GAUGE	LENGTH	
SHAPE NAME			
ANATOMY	FILLER		
BINDER		WRAPPER	
APPEARANCE			

CONSTRUCTION

DRAW	START	1/2	3/4
BURN	START	1/2	3/4

TASTING NOTES

OTHER NOTES

EVALUATION

O O O O O O O O O O

POOR   CLASSIC

RECOMMEND AND ENJOY AGAIN?   Y   N

Cigar Log Entry

MINUTIAE	DATE	OCCASION	
BRAND			PRICE
VITOLA	GAUGE	LENGTH	
SHAPE NAME			
ANATOMY	FILLER		
BINDER		WRAPPER	
APPEARANCE			
CONSTRUCTION			

DRAW	START	1/2	3/4
BURN	START	1/2	3/4

TASTING NOTES

OTHER NOTES

EVALUATION

○ ○ ○ ○ ○ ○ ○ ○ ○ ○

POOR   CLASSIC

RECOMMEND AND ENJOY AGAIN?   Y   N

ATTACH BAND HERE

Cigar Log Entry

ATTACH BAND HERE

MINUTIAE	DATE	OCCASION		
BRAND			PRICE	
VITOLA	GAUGE		LENGTH	
SHAPE NAME				
ANATOMY	FILLER			
BINDER		WRAPPER		
APPEARANCE				
CONSTRUCTION				
DRAW	START	1/2	3/4	
BURN	START	1/2	3/4	
TASTING NOTES				
OTHER NOTES				

EVALUATION

O O O O O O O O O O

POOR   CLASSIC

RECOMMEND AND ENJOY AGAIN?   Y   N

Cigar Log Entry

MINUTIAE	DATE		OCCASION		
BRAND					PRICE
VITOLA	GAUGE		LENGTH		
SHAPE NAME					
ANATOMY	FILLER				
BINDER			WRAPPER		

APPEARANCE

CONSTRUCTION

DRAW	START	1/2	3/4
BURN	START	1/2	3/4

TASTING NOTES

OTHER NOTES

EVALUATION

◯ ◯ ◯ ◯ ◯ ◯ ◯ ◯ ◯ ◯

POOR   CLASSIC

RECOMMEND AND ENJOY AGAIN?   Y   N

ATTACH BAND HERE

Cigar Log Entry

ATTACH BAND HERE

MINUTIAE	DATE		OCCASION	
BRAND				PRICE
VITOLA	GAUGE		LENGTH	
SHAPE NAME				
ANATOMY	FILLER			
BINDER			WRAPPER	
APPEARANCE				

CONSTRUCTION

DRAW	START	1/2	3/4
BURN	START	1/2	3/4

TASTING NOTES

OTHER NOTES

EVALUATION

O O O O O O O O O O

POOR   CLASSIC

RECOMMEND AND ENJOY AGAIN?   Y   N

Cigar Log Entry

MINUTIAE	DATE		OCCASION		
BRAND					PRICE
VITOLA	GAUGE			LENGTH	
SHAPE NAME					
ANATOMY	FILLER				
BINDER			WRAPPER		
APPEARANCE					
CONSTRUCTION					

DRAW	START	1/2	3/4
BURN	START	1/2	3/4

TASTING NOTES

OTHER NOTES

EVALUATION

○ ○ ○ ○ ○ ○ ○ ○ ○ ○

POOR　　　　　　　　　　　　　　　　　　　　　CLASSIC

RECOMMEND AND ENJOY AGAIN?　　Y　　N

ATTACH BAND HERE

Cigar Log Entry

ATTACH BAND HERE

MINUTIAE	DATE		OCCASION	
BRAND				PRICE
VITOLA	GAUGE		LENGTH	
SHAPE NAME				
ANATOMY	FILLER			
BINDER			WRAPPER	
APPEARANCE				

CONSTRUCTION

DRAW	START	1/2	3/4
BURN	START	1/2	3/4

TASTING NOTES

OTHER NOTES

EVALUATION

O O O O O O O O O O

POOR   CLASSIC

RECOMMEND AND ENJOY AGAIN?   Y   N

Cigar Log Entry

MINUTIAE	DATE		OCCASION		
BRAND					PRICE
VITOLA	GAUGE		LENGTH		
SHAPE NAME					
ANATOMY	FILLER				
BINDER			WRAPPER		

APPEARANCE

CONSTRUCTION

DRAW	START		1/2		3/4
BURN	START		1/2		3/4

TASTING NOTES

OTHER NOTES

EVALUATION

O O O O O O O O O O

POOR   CLASSIC

RECOMMEND AND ENJOY AGAIN?   Y   N

ATTACH BAND HERE

Cigar Log Entry

ATTACH BAND HERE

MINUTIAE	DATE	OCCASION	

BRAND			PRICE

VITOLA	GAUGE		LENGTH

SHAPE NAME

ANATOMY	FILLER	

BINDER		WRAPPER

APPEARANCE

CONSTRUCTION

DRAW	START	1/2	3/4
BURN	START	1/2	3/4

TASTING NOTES

OTHER NOTES

EVALUATION

O O O O O O O O O O

POOR   CLASSIC

RECOMMEND AND ENJOY AGAIN?   Y   N

Cigar Log Entry

MINUTIAE	DATE	OCCASION	
BRAND			PRICE
VITOLA	GAUGE	LENGTH	
SHAPE NAME			
ANATOMY	FILLER		
BINDER		WRAPPER	

APPEARANCE

CONSTRUCTION

DRAW	START	1/2	3/4
BURN	START	1/2	3/4

TASTING NOTES

OTHER NOTES

EVALUATION

O O O O O O O O O O

POOR   CLASSIC

RECOMMEND AND ENJOY AGAIN?   Y   N

ATTACH BAND HERE

Cigar Log Entry

ATTACH BAND HERE

MINUTIAE	DATE	OCCASION	

BRAND		PRICE

VITOLA	GAUGE	LENGTH

SHAPE NAME

ANATOMY	FILLER

BINDER	WRAPPER

APPEARANCE

CONSTRUCTION

DRAW	START	1/2	3/4
BURN	START	1/2	3/4

TASTING NOTES

OTHER NOTES

EVALUATION

○ ○ ○ ○ ○ ○ ○ ○ ○ ○

POOR   CLASSIC

RECOMMEND AND ENJOY AGAIN?   Y   N

Cigar Log Entry

MINUTIAE	DATE		OCCASION		
BRAND				PRICE	
VITOLA	GAUGE		LENGTH		
SHAPE NAME					
ANATOMY	FILLER				
BINDER			WRAPPER		

APPEARANCE

CONSTRUCTION

DRAW	START	1/2	3/4
BURN	START	1/2	3/4

TASTING NOTES

OTHER NOTES

EVALUATION

O O O O O O O O O O

POOR   CLASSIC

RECOMMEND AND ENJOY AGAIN?   Y   N

ATTACH BAND HERE

Cigar Log Entry

ATTACH BAND HERE

MINUTIAE	DATE		OCCASION	
BRAND				PRICE
VITOLA	GAUGE		LENGTH	
SHAPE NAME				
ANATOMY	FILLER			
BINDER			WRAPPER	
APPEARANCE				
CONSTRUCTION				
DRAW	START	1/2		3/4
BURN	START	1/2		3/4
TASTING NOTES				
OTHER NOTES				

EVALUATION

O   O   O   O   O   O   O   O   O   O

POOR   CLASSIC

RECOMMEND AND ENJOY AGAIN?   Y   N

Cigar Log Entry

MINUTIAE	DATE	OCCASION	
BRAND			PRICE
VITOLA	GAUGE	LENGTH	
SHAPE NAME			
ANATOMY	FILLER		
BINDER		WRAPPER	

APPEARANCE

CONSTRUCTION

DRAW	START	1/2	3/4
BURN	START	1/2	3/4

TASTING NOTES

OTHER NOTES

EVALUATION

O O O O O O O O O O

POOR   CLASSIC

RECOMMEND AND ENJOY AGAIN?   Y   N

ATTACH BAND HERE

Cigar Log Entry

ATTACH BAND HERE

MINUTIAE	DATE		OCCASION	
BRAND				PRICE
VITOLA	GAUGE		LENGTH	
SHAPE NAME				
ANATOMY	FILLER			
BINDER			WRAPPER	

APPEARANCE

CONSTRUCTION

DRAW	START	1/2	3/4
BURN	START	1/2	3/4

TASTING NOTES

OTHER NOTES

EVALUATION

○ ○ ○ ○ ○ ○ ○ ○ ○ ○

POOR   CLASSIC

RECOMMEND AND ENJOY AGAIN?   Y   N

Cigar Log Entry

MINUTIAE	DATE		OCCASION		
BRAND					PRICE
VITOLA	GAUGE			LENGTH	
SHAPE NAME					
ANATOMY	FILLER				
BINDER				WRAPPER	

APPEARANCE

CONSTRUCTION

DRAW	START	1/2	3/4
BURN	START	1/2	3/4

TASTING NOTES

OTHER NOTES

EVALUATION

○ ○ ○ ○ ○ ○ ○ ○ ○ ○

POOR   CLASSIC

RECOMMEND AND ENJOY AGAIN?   **Y**   **N**

ATTACH BAND HERE

Cigar Log Entry

ATTACH BAND HERE

MINUTIAE	DATE		OCCASION		
BRAND					PRICE
VITOLA	GAUGE		LENGTH		
SHAPE NAME					
ANATOMY	FILLER				
BINDER			WRAPPER		
APPEARANCE					

CONSTRUCTION

DRAW	START	1/2	3/4
BURN	START	1/2	3/4

TASTING NOTES

OTHER NOTES

EVALUATION

O O O O O O O O O O

POOR CLASSIC

RECOMMEND AND ENJOY AGAIN? Y N

Cigar Log Entry

MINUTIAE	DATE	OCCASION	
BRAND			PRICE
VITOLA	GAUGE	LENGTH	
SHAPE NAME			
ANATOMY	FILLER		
BINDER		WRAPPER	
APPEARANCE			

CONSTRUCTION

DRAW	START	1/2	3/4
BURN	START	1/2	3/4

TASTING NOTES

OTHER NOTES

EVALUATION

○ ○ ○ ○ ○ ○ ○ ○ ○ ○

POOR   CLASSIC

RECOMMEND AND ENJOY AGAIN?   Y   N

ATTACH BAND HERE

Cigar Log Entry

ATTACH BAND HERE

MINUTIAE	DATE		OCCASION		
BRAND					PRICE
VITOLA	GAUGE		LENGTH		
SHAPE NAME					
ANATOMY	FILLER				
BINDER			WRAPPER		
APPEARANCE					
CONSTRUCTION					

DRAW	START	1/2	3/4
BURN	START	1/2	3/4

TASTING NOTES

OTHER NOTES

EVALUATION

O O O O O O O O O O

POOR   CLASSIC

RECOMMEND AND ENJOY AGAIN?   Y   N

Cigar Log Entry

MINUTIAE	DATE	OCCASION		
BRAND				PRICE
VITOLA	GAUGE		LENGTH	
SHAPE NAME				
ANATOMY	FILLER			
BINDER		WRAPPER		

APPEARANCE

CONSTRUCTION

DRAW	START	1/2	3/4
BURN	START	1/2	3/4

TASTING NOTES

OTHER NOTES

EVALUATION

O O O O O O O O O O

POOR   CLASSIC

RECOMMEND AND ENJOY AGAIN?   Y   N

ATTACH BAND HERE

Cigar Log Entry

ATTACH BAND HERE

MINUTIAE	DATE	OCCASION		
BRAND			PRICE	
VITOLA	GAUGE		LENGTH	
SHAPE NAME				
ANATOMY	FILLER			
BINDER			WRAPPER	
APPEARANCE				
CONSTRUCTION				

DRAW	START	1/2	3/4
BURN	START	1/2	3/4

TASTING NOTES

OTHER NOTES

EVALUATION

O O O O O O O O O O

POOR   CLASSIC

RECOMMEND AND ENJOY AGAIN?   Y   N

Cigar Log Entry

MINUTIAE	DATE		OCCASION		
BRAND				PRICE	
VITOLA	GAUGE		LENGTH		
SHAPE NAME					
ANATOMY	FILLER				
BINDER			WRAPPER		
APPEARANCE					
CONSTRUCTION					
DRAW	START		1/2		3/4
BURN	START		1/2		3/4

TASTING NOTES

OTHER NOTES

EVALUATION

O O O O O O O O O O

POOR   CLASSIC

RECOMMEND AND ENJOY AGAIN?   Y   N

ATTACH BAND HERE

Cigar Log Entry

ATTACH BAND HERE

MINUTIAE	DATE		OCCASION		
BRAND				PRICE	
VITOLA	GAUGE		LENGTH		
SHAPE NAME					
ANATOMY	FILLER				
BINDER			WRAPPER		
APPEARANCE					

CONSTRUCTION				
DRAW	START	1/2	3/4	
BURN	START	1/2	3/4	

TASTING NOTES

OTHER NOTES

EVALUATION

O O O O O O O O O O

POOR　　　　　　　　　　　　　　　　　　CLASSIC

RECOMMEND AND ENJOY AGAIN?　　Y　　N

Cigar Log Entry

MINUTIAE	DATE		OCCASION		
BRAND					PRICE
VITOLA	GAUGE		LENGTH		
SHAPE NAME					
ANATOMY	FILLER				
BINDER			WRAPPER		
APPEARANCE					
CONSTRUCTION					

DRAW	START	1/2	3/4
BURN	START	1/2	3/4

TASTING NOTES

OTHER NOTES

EVALUATION

◯ ◯ ◯ ◯ ◯ ◯ ◯ ◯ ◯ ◯

POOR   CLASSIC

RECOMMEND AND ENJOY AGAIN?   Y   N

ATTACH BAND HERE

Cigar Log Entry

ATTACH BAND HERE

MINUTIAE	DATE	OCCASION	
BRAND			PRICE
VITOLA	GAUGE	LENGTH	
SHAPE NAME			
ANATOMY	FILLER		
BINDER		WRAPPER	
APPEARANCE			
CONSTRUCTION			

DRAW	START	1/2	3/4
BURN	START	1/2	3/4

TASTING NOTES

OTHER NOTES

EVALUATION

O O O O O O O O O O

POOR   CLASSIC

RECOMMEND AND ENJOY AGAIN?   Y   N

Cigar Log Entry

MINUTIAE	DATE	OCCASION	
BRAND			PRICE
VITOLA	GAUGE	LENGTH	
SHAPE NAME			
ANATOMY	FILLER		
BINDER		WRAPPER	
APPEARANCE			
CONSTRUCTION			

DRAW	START	1/2	3/4
BURN	START	1/2	3/4

TASTING NOTES

OTHER NOTES

EVALUATION

◯ ◯ ◯ ◯ ◯ ◯ ◯ ◯ ◯ ◯

POOR   CLASSIC

RECOMMEND AND ENJOY AGAIN?   Y   N

ATTACH BAND HERE

Cigar Log Entry

ATTACH BAND HERE

MINUTIAE	DATE	OCCASION	

BRAND			PRICE

VITOLA	GAUGE	LENGTH	

SHAPE NAME

ANATOMY	FILLER

BINDER	WRAPPER

APPEARANCE

CONSTRUCTION

DRAW	START	1/2	3/4
BURN	START	1/2	3/4

TASTING NOTES

OTHER NOTES

EVALUATION

O O O O O O O O O O

POOR   CLASSIC

RECOMMEND AND ENJOY AGAIN?   Y   N

Cigar Log Entry

MINUTIAE	DATE		OCCASION		
BRAND					PRICE
VITOLA	GAUGE		LENGTH		
SHAPE NAME					
ANATOMY	FILLER				
BINDER			WRAPPER		

APPEARANCE

CONSTRUCTION

DRAW	START	1/2	3/4
BURN	START	1/2	3/4

TASTING NOTES

OTHER NOTES

EVALUATION

○ ○ ○ ○ ○ ○ ○ ○ ○ ○

POOR   CLASSIC

RECOMMEND AND ENJOY AGAIN?   Y   N

ATTACH BAND HERE

Cigar Log Entry

ATTACH BAND HERE

MINUTIAE	DATE		OCCASION		
BRAND				PRICE	
VITOLA	GAUGE		LENGTH		
SHAPE NAME					
ANATOMY	FILLER				
BINDER			WRAPPER		
APPEARANCE					

CONSTRUCTION

DRAW	START	1/2	3/4
BURN	START	1/2	3/4

TASTING NOTES

OTHER NOTES

EVALUATION

O O O O O O O O O O

POOR   CLASSIC

RECOMMEND AND ENJOY AGAIN?   Y   N

Cigar Log Entry

MINUTIAE	DATE	OCCASION	
BRAND			PRICE
VITOLA	GAUGE	LENGTH	
SHAPE NAME			
ANATOMY	FILLER		
BINDER		WRAPPER	

APPEARANCE

CONSTRUCTION

DRAW	START	1/2	3/4
BURN	START	1/2	3/4

TASTING NOTES

OTHER NOTES

EVALUATION

O   O   O   O   O   O   O   O   O   O

POOR   CLASSIC

RECOMMEND AND ENJOY AGAIN?   Y   N

ATTACH BAND HERE

Index of Cigar Entries

Use the Index of Cigar Entries pages to write the names of the cigars you have tasted according to the page numbers listed. Indicate whether you recommended the cigar or not in the Rec column (Y = yes and N = no) and give the body of the cigar (L = light/mild, M = medium or F = full) in the Body column.

Pg #	Cigar Manufacturer / Name	Rec Y/N	Body L/M/F
10			
11			
12			
13			
14			
15			
16			
17			
18			
19			
20			
21			
22			
23			
24			
25			
26			
27			
28			
29			
30			

Pg #	Cigar Manufacturer / Name	Rec Y/N	Body L/M/F
31			
32			
33			
34			
35			
36			
37			
38			
39			
40			
41			
42			
43			
44			
45			
46			
47			
48			
49			
50			
51			
52			
53			
54			
55			
56			

Pg #	Cigar Manufacturer / Name	Rec Y/N	Body L/M/F
57			
58			
59			
60			
61			
62			
63			
64			
65			
66			
67			
68			
69			
70			
71			
72			
73			
74			
75			
76			
77			
78			
79			
80			
81			
82			

Pg #	Cigar Manufacturer / Name	Rec Y/N	Body L/M/F
83			
84			
85			
86			
87			
88			
89			
90			
91			
92			
93			
94			
95			
96			
97			
98			
99			
100			
101			
102			
103			
104			
105			
106			
107			
108			

Pg #	Cigar Name / Manufacturer	Rec Y/N	Body L/M/F
109			
110			
111			
112			
113			
114			
115			
116			
117			
118			
119			
120			
121			
122			
123			
124			
125			
126			
127			
128			
129			
130			
131			
132			
133			
134			

CIGAR GAUGES AND RULER

A cigar's ring gauge is measured in 64ths of an inch. Thus, a cigar with a gauge of 64 is 1 inch in diameter. Use this page to determine your cigar's gauge and length.

Made in the USA
Monee, IL
12 July 2020